1. Introduction

The unique characteristics of animals is a miscellany of facts, genuine or supposed, gleamed from earlier and contemporary Greek writers (No Latin writer is once named) and to a limited extent from his own observation to illustrate the habits of the animal world.

We are of course prepared to encounter much that modern science rejects, but the general tone with its search after the picturesque, the startling, even the miraculous, would justify us in ranking Aelian with the paradoxical, rather than with the sober exponents of natural history.

Mythology, mariners' yarns, vulgar superstitions, the ascertained facts of nature—all serve to adorn a tale and, on occasion, to point a moral. His religion is the popular stoicism of the age. Aleian repeatedly affirms his belief in the gods and in divine providence; the wisdom and beneficence of Nature are held up to veneration; the folly and selfishness of man are contrasted with the untaught virtues of the animal world. Some animals, to be sure, have their failings, but he chooses rather to dwell upon their good qualities, devotion, courage, self-sacrifice, gratitude. Again, animals are guided by reason, and from them we may learn contentment, control of the passions, and calm in the face of death.

His primary object is to entertain and while so doing to convey instruction in the most agreeable form. Some might find fault with his random and piece-meal handling of his theme-of which he is well aware, and he defends himself with the plea that a frequent change of topic helps to maintain the reader's interest and saves him from boredom.

As to the permanent value of his work he has no misgivings and since we have been informed that his writings were much admired, we may assume that they appealed to cultivated circles in a way that the voluminous and possibly arid compilations of grammarians did not.

Now I am well aware of the labour that others have expended on this subject, yet I have collected all the materials that I could; I have clothed them in untechnical language, and am persuaded that my achievement is a treasure far from negligible. So if anyone considers them profitable, let him make use of them; anyone who does not consider them so may give them to his father to keep and attend to.

Animal Peculiarity Volume 3 Part 5

By T.P Just

~~~

Copyright © 2010 by Terence Just. All rights reserved.

Get All The Books In The Series:

Animal Peculiarity Volume 1 Part [1-8]
Animal Peculiarity Volume 2 Part [1-8]
Animal Peculiarity Volume 3 Part [1-8]
Just Enterprises

Table of Contents

2. Music and the Elephant

These two accounts from India and Libya show a difference. The Indian shall relate the practice in his country, and the Libyan shall relate what he knows. So their two accounts are as follows. In India if a full-grown Elephant is captured he is hard to tame and his craving for freedom makes him thirst for blood, and if you make him fast with ropes his anger is inflamed all the more and he will not stand being a slave and a prisoner.

But the Indians blandish him with .food and try to mollify him with a variety of attractive baits, offering him what will fill his stomach and assuage his passion: Yet he is displeased with them and takes no notice of them. So what device do the Indians adopt to meet this?

They introduce native music and charm the Elephants with a musical instrument that is in common use; it is called scindapsus. And the Elephant lends an ear and is pacified, his rage is softened, and his passion is subdued and allayed, and little by little he begins to notice his food.

Then he is freed from his bonds but remains captivated by the music, and.-eats his food with the eagerness of a man faring sumptuously: for in his love for the music he will no longer run away.

3. The Libyan Mare

But the mares of Libya (for we must listen to the second account as well) are equally captivated by the sound of the pipe. They become gentle and tame and cease to prance and be skittish, and follow the herdsman wherever the music leads them; and if he stands still, so do they.
But if he plays his pipe with greater vigour, tears of pleasure stream from their eyes. Now the herdsmen of the mares hollow a stick of rose-laurel, fashion it into a pipe, and blow into it, and thereby charm the aforesaid animals.
And Euripides speaks of some 'marriage songs of shepherds' this is the pipe-music which throws mares into an amorous frenzy and makes horses mad with desire to couple. This in fact is how the mating of horses is brought about, and the pipe-music seems to provide a marriage song.

4. Arion and the Dolphins

Sufficient proof that Dolphins love song and Arian and the music of pipes is supplied by Arlon of Methymna the Dolphins in his statue on Taenarum and the inscription written upon it. The inscription runs.

> 'Sent by the immortals this mount saved Arlon son of Cycleus from the Sicilian main.'

And Arlon wrote a hymn of thanks to Poseidon that bears witness to the Dolphins' love of music and is a kind of payment of the reward due to them also for having saved his life.

This is the hymn.

> 'Highest of the gods, lord of the sea, Poseidon of the golden trident, earth-shaker in the swelling brine, around thee the finny monster in a ring swim and dance, with nimble flinging of their • feet leaping lightly, snub-nosed hounds with . bristling neck, swift .runners, music-loving • dolphins, sea-nurslings of the Nereid maids divine, whom Amphitrite bore, even they that carried me, a wanderer on the Sicilian main, to the headland of Taenarum in Pelops' land, mounting me upon their humped backs as they clove the furrow of Nereus' plain, a

path untrodden, when deceitful men had cast -Me from their sea-faring hollow ship into the purple swell Of ocean.

SO to the characteristics of dolphins mentioned earlier on I think we may add a love of music.

5. Music As The Means Of Capturing Animals

There is an Etruscan story current which says music as a that the wild boars and the stags in that country are caught by Using nets and hounds, as is the usual Animals manner of hunting, but that music plays a- part, and even the larger part, in the struggle.

And how this happens I will now relate: - They set the nets and other hunting gear that ensnare the animals in a circle, and a man proficient on the pipes stands there and tries his utmost to play a rather soft tune, avoiding any shriller note, but playing the sweetest melodies possible.

The quiet and the stillness easily carry the sound abroad; and the music streams up to the heights and into ravines and thickets in a word into every lair and resting-place of these animals. Now at first when the sound penetrates to their ears it strikes them with terror and fills them with dread, and then an unalloyed and irresistible delight in the music takes hold of them, and they are so beguiled as to forget about their offspring and their homes.

And yet wild beasts do not care to wander away from their native haunts. But little by little these creatures in Etruria are attracted as though by some persuasive spell, and beneath the wizardry of the music they come and fall into the snares, overpowered by the melody.

6. The Anthias Fish

The Anthias, if wounded while it is being captured, is a most pitiful sight, and as it dies seems to be mourning for itself and to be somehow imploring, like men who have fallen among pitiless and most bloodthirsty brigands.

For some of these fish in their attempt to escape get entangled in the nets, and as they try to leap out of the ambush are caught by the harpoon. Others which contrive to escape this death, spring out on to the shore, hitherto the fishes' enemy, preferring, and gladly so, death with-out the aid of the sword.

Gordius and an Eagle

I have heard that an eagle intimated to Gordius and that his son Midas would be king when ,as he was an Eagle ploughing, it flew over Gordius, and then settling upon the yoke, remained with him all day long and did not depart before he finished his ploughing at eventide when the hour for unyoking was at hand.

Gelon and a Wolf

And when Gelon of Syracuse was a boy an immense wolf sprang into the schoolroom and with its teeth snatched his writing-tablet from his hands. And Gelon rose from his seat and gave chase, not being afraid of the beast but clinging valiantly to his writing-tablet.

And when he got outside the schoolroom it fell and crushed the boys along with the master. It was by divine providence that Gelon was the only one to escape.

And the strange thing is that the wolf did not kill a man but saved his life, for the gods did not disdain to foreshow a kingdom to one even by means of a dumb animal, and to save the other from danger that threatened.

So it is characteristic of animals to be beloved of the gods.

The Sargue

This is how the people of Carla catch Sargues. When the south wind is blowing gently and sending softer breezes and when the waves are at rest and chime lightly upon the sands, then the fisherman has no need of his reed, but taking a rod of very tough juniper he fastens a cord on the end and spits a half pickled anchovy on the hook and lets it down into the sea.

And he sits in the prow of the skiff and dangles the lure, while his boy rows gently, having purposely been instructed beforehand in the art of leisurely propulsion, and makes the skiff move in the direction of the shore. And the Sargues dart up in their numbers from their native lairs and gambol around and collect about the hook.

For the- fish, long dead indeed but prepared for catching, draws them as it were with a spell. Presently when they are close to the shore they are easily caught, being made prisoners through their belly's greed.

Fishes their haunts and their foods

The haunts of fishes are numerous : some are found among rocks, others in sand, others again their food among vegetation, for you must know there is vegetation even in the sea, and some is called 'oyster-green, some' vines', certain kinds' grapes,' and others ' grass-wrack.'

And it seems that the name cabbage also is attached to marine vegetation, and some kinds are called' seaweed,' and some' hair.' And some fish feed on one kind, others on another, .and a fish that is accustomed to the food on which it has been reared and to which it is, so to say, akin would never touch any other kind.

7. The Star gazer fish

You may hear fishermen speak also of a fish they call Callionymus (Star-gazer). And concerning it Aristotle says that it has a considerable quantity of gall·stored close to the right-hand lobe of the liver, and that its liver is situated on its left side. And Menander bears witness to these statements when he says in his Messenian woman:

I will make you have more gall than a Star-gazer and Anaxippus in his Epidicazomenus

If you rouse me and make all my gall boil like a Star-gazer's, you will find that I differ no whit from a sword-fish.'

There are those who assert that it is edible; most people however assert the contrary. But you will not easily discover any mention of the Star-gazer in any description of fish-banquet, although poets have been at pains to record every fish of any value.; they are Epicharmus in his Hebe' s Wedding his Land and Sea and also his Muses and Mnesimachus in his Isthmian Victor.

The Fishing frog

The Fishing -frog also lays an egg, as birds do, for it is not viviparous, because its new-born young have a large, rough head, and for that reason it is incapable of taking them back when they are frightened. For their re-entry will lacerate and injure the parent, and were they to be born alive and to emerge so, they would produce the same effect.

And so they are not well adapted to producing their young alive nor are they a secure place of refuge for them. The egg of the Fishing-frog does not conform to the nature and character of an egg, for even that is rough and has scales, and you will find it hard if you touch it.

8. A Monstrous Octopus

Octopuses naturally, with the lapse of time, attain to enormous proportions and approach cetaceans and are actually reckoned as such. At any rate I learn of an octopus at Dicaearchia in Italy which attained to a monstrous bulk and scorned and despised food from the sea and such pasturage as it provided.

And so this creature actually came out on to the land and seized things there. Now it swam up through a subterranean sewer that discharged the refuse of the aforesaid city into the sea and emerged in a house on the shore where some Iberian merchants had their cargo, that is, pickled fish from that country in immense jars: it threw its tentacles round the earthenware vessels and with its grip broke them and feasted on the pickled fish.

And when the merchants entered and saw the broken pieces, they realised that a large quantity of their cargo had disappeared ; and they were amazed and could not guess who had robbed them : they saw that no attempt had been made upon the doors ; the roof was undamaged ; the walls had not been broken through.

They saw also the remains of the pickled fish that had been left behind by the uninvited guest. So they decided to have their most courageous servant armed and waiting in ambush in the house. Well, during the night the Octopus crept up to its accustomed meal and clasping the vessels, as an athlete puts a strangle-hold upon his adversary, with all his might gripping firmly, the robber — if I may so call the Octopus — crushed the earthenware with the greatest ease.

It was full moon, and the house was full of light, and everything was quite visible. But the servant was not for attacking the brute single-handed as he was afraid, moreover his adversary was too big for one man, but in the morning he informed the merchants what had happened. They could not believe their ears.

Then some of them remembering how heavily they had been mulcted, were for risking the danger and were eager to encounter their enemy, while others in their thirst for this singular and incredible spectacle voluntarily shut themselves up with their companions in order to help them.

Later, in the evening the marauder paid his visit and made for his usual feast. Thereupon some of them closed off the conduit; others took arms against the enemy and with choppers and razors well sharpened cut the tentacles, just as vine-dressers and woodmen lop the tips of the branches of an oak.

And having cut away its strength, at long last they overcame it not without considerable labour. And what was so strange was that merchants captured the fish on dry land. Mischief and craft are plainly seen to be characteristics of this creature.

9. Remedies for sick Elephants

The people of India heal the wounds of Elephants which they
have captured in the following manner. They foment them
with warm water, just as Patroclus fomented the wound of
EnrypyluS in our noble Homer and then anoint them with
butter. But if they are deep, they reduce the inflammation by
applying and laying on them pigs' flesh hot and with the
blood still in it.

Their ophthalmia they treat by warming some cow's milk and
pouring it into their eyes, and the Elephants open their eyelids
and are gratified just as men are, to perceive what benefit they
derive.

And the Indians continue the bathing until the inflammation
ceases; this is evidence that the ophthalmia has been arrested.
As for other diseases that afflict them, black wine is the cure
for them. But if this medicine does not rid them of their
complaint, then nothing will save them.

The Elephant and its love of flowers

An Elephant belonging to a herd but which has been tamed drinks water; but an Elephant that fights in war drinks wine, not however that made from grapes, for men prepare a wine from rice from cane.

And these tame Elephants go out to gather flowers for themselves, for they love a sweet smell and are led to the meadows to be trained by the most fragrant scent. And an Elephant using its sense of smell will pick out a flower, while the trainer, basket in hand, holds it out beneath the picker as he throws it in. Later when it has filled the basket, like a fruit-gatherer it has a bath and takes as much pleasure in the bath as the more luxurious of mankind do.

Then on its return it wants the flowers, and if the keeper delays, it trumpets and refuses food until somebody brings it the flowers it has gathered. Then it picks them out of the basket with its trunk and sprinkles them along the rim of its manger, for it regards them as imparting a flavour, as it were, to its food by means of their scent.

And it scatters a quantity of flowers over its stall, as it desires a fragrant sleep. It seems that Indian Elephants are nine cubits high and five wide, and the largest are those they call Prasian; next to these one may reckon those from Taxila

.

10. The Indian Horse

To control an Indian Horse, to check him when he leaps forward and would gallop away, has not, it seems, been given to every man, but only to those who have been brought up from childhood to manage horses.

For it is not the Indian custom to rule them, to bring them to order, and to direct them by means of the rein but by spiked muzzles; thus their tongue goes unpunished and the roof of their mouth untormented.

Still, those who are skilled in horseman-ship compel them to go round and round, returning to the same point. Now if a man would do this he requires strength of hand and a thorough under-standing of horses. Those who have attained the summit of this science even try by these means to drive a chariot in circles.

And it would be no contemptible achievement to make a team of four ravenous horses circle about with ease. And the chariot holds two beside the driver.

The War Elephant

But a War elephant in what is called the tower, or even, assure you, on its bare back, free of harness, carries as many as three armed men. . . . Who hurl their weapons to left and right, and a third behind them, while a fourth holds the goad with which he controls the beast, as a helmsman or pilot of a vessel controls a ship with the rudder.

11. Leopard-hunting in Mauretania

The hunting of Leopards seems to be a Moorish practice; The people build a stone structure, and it resembles a kind of cage : this is the first part of the ambush; and the second part is this: inside they fasten a piece of meat that has gone bad and smells, by a longish cord and set up a flimsy door made of plaited reeds of some kind, and through them the smell of the aforesaid meat is exhaled and spreads abroad.

The animals notice it, being for some reason fond of ill-smelling objects, because the scent from them assails them whether they are on mountain tops or in a ravine or even in a glen. Then when the Leopard encounters the smell it gets excited and in its excessive desire comes rushing to the feast it loves : it is drawn to it as though by some spell:

Then it dashes at the door, knocks it down, and fastens upon the fatal meal-fatal, because on to the aforesaid cord there has been woven a noose most dexterously contrived, and as the meat is being eaten this is dislodged and encircles the gluttonous Leopard.

So it is caught and pays the penalty for its ravenous belly and its foul feasting, the poor wretch.

12. Fox and Hare

Hares are caught by Foxes more often than not through an artifice, for the Fox is a master of trickery and knows many a ruse. For instance, when by night it comes upon the track of a Hare and has scented the animal, it steals upon it softly and with noiseless tread, and holds its breath, and finding it in its form, attempts to seize it, supposing it to be free of fear and anxiety.

But the Hare is not a luxurious creature and does not sleep carefree, but directly it is aware of the Fox's approach it leaps from its bed and is off. And it speeds on its way with all haste: but the Fox follows in its track and continues its pursuit. And the Hare after covering a great distance, under the impression that it has won and is not likely to be caught, plunges into a thicket and is glad to rest.

But the Fox is after it and will not allow it to remain still, but once again rouses it and stimulates it to run again. Then a second course no shorter than the first is gone through, and the Hare again longs to rest, but the Fox is upon it and by shaking the thicket contrives to keep it from sleeping. And again it darts out, but the Fox is hard after it. But when it is driven into running course after course without inter-mission, and want of sleep ensues, the Hare gives up and the Fox overtakes it and seizes it, having caught it not indeed by speed but by length of time and by craft.

13. The Hare

It seems that the Hare knows about winds and seasons, for it is a sagacious creature. During the winter it makes its bed in sunny spots, for it obviously likes to be warm and hates the cold. But in summer time it prefers a northern aspect, wishing to be cool. Its nostrils, like a sundial, mark the variation of the seasons.

The Hare does not close its eyes when sleeping: this advantage over other animals it alone enjoys and its eyelids are never overcome by slumber. They say that it sleeps with its body alone while it continues to see with its eyes.

(I am only writing -what experienced hunters say.) Its time for feeding: is at night, which may be because it desires unfamiliar food, though I should say that it was for the sake of exercise, in order that, while refraining from sleep all this time and full of activity, it may improve its speed.

But it greatly likes to return to its home and loves every spot with which it is familiar. That, you see, is why it is generally caught, because it cannot endure to abandon its native haunts.

14. The Hare of the plains

The Hare when pursued by hounds and horse men runs, if it is a denizen of the plains, swifter than of the Mountain Hare, as its body is small and slim. Hence it is not unnatural for it to be nimble. At any rate to begin with it leaps and bounds from the earth and slips through thickets and across marshy ground with ease, and wherever the grass is deep it escapes without difficulty.

And just as they say that the tail of the lion can rouse and stimulate it, so it is with the ears of the Hare : they are signals for speed and excite it to run. At any rate it lays them back and uses them as goads to prevent it from lagging and hesitating. But its course is not, uniform and straight,, but it turns aside now right now left and doubles this way and that, bewildering and deluding the hounds.

And in whatever direction it wants to swerve in its course, it droops one ear, to that avenue of escape, as though it were steering its course, therewith: It does not however squander its powers, but observes the pace of its pursuer, and if he is tardy, it does not put forth its whole strength but keeps itself in check somewhat, enough to outrun the hound but not enough to exhaust Itself by intense speed..

For it knows that it can run faster and realises that this is not the moment for it to over-exert itself. If however the hound is very swift; then the Hare runs as fast as its feet can carry it. And when at length it has got far ahead and has left hunters, hounds, and horsemen a long way behind, it races up some high hill and sitting up on its hind legs surveys as from a watch-tower the efforts of its pursuers and, as I think, laughs at them for being feebler than itself.

Then emboldened by the advantage it has gained, like one who has achieved peace and calm, it is glad to rest and lies down to sleep.

15. The Hare of the Mountains

The Mountain Hares, however, are not so swift as those that live in the plains, unless indeed the former also have plain-land lying below into which they can descend and run about. Though their home is on a mountain they exercise themselves in the plain, often running about with the Hares there.
The usual thing when they are pursued in the plain is for them to start up and to lie hid by turns, but since they are constantly forced out, not one escapes.
But when they are on the point of being caught they change suddenly their direction over the plain and dart uphill into the mountains, speeding of course to their native haunts, their proper domain; and in this way they escape and are gone, reaching unexpected safety, for horses and hounds dislike going up mountains, since their feet give out and are very quickly worn down, while hounds suffer even worse, their paws being fleshy and having nothing to resist the rocks, as horses have their hooves.
The Hare on the contrary has naturally hairy paws and is quite content with rough ground.

16. The Rabbit

There is also another kind of Hare, small by nature, and it never grows larger. It is called a Rabbit. I am no inventor of names, which is the reason why in this account I preserve the original name given to it by the Iberians of the west in whose country the Rabbit is produced in great numbers.

Its colour compared with that of hares is dark; it has a small tail, but in other respects it is like them. A further difference is in the size of its head, for it is smaller and curiously scant of flesh and shorter.

But it is more lustful than the hare . . . which cause it to go raving mad when it goes after the female. [The stag also has a bone in its heart, and someone else shall make it his business to discover what purpose it selves.

17. Fishing for Tunny

The pursuit of the Tunny is commonly designated as' big fishing' by the people of Italy and Sicily, and the places in which they are in the habit of storing their huge nets and other fishing gear are called 'big-fishing tackle stores,' for they wish henceforward to segregate the huge Tunny into the class of ' big fishes.'

And I learn that the Celts and the people of Massalia and all those in Liguria catch Tunny with hooks, but these must be made of iron and of great size and stout. So much then for Tunnies in addition to what I have already said earlier on.

18. The 'Aulopias' fish

Those who are in the habit of fishing round the Tyrrhenian islands as they are called, hunt a gigantic fish which they call the Aulopias, and it is worthwhile to describe its characteristics. In the matter of size the largest Aulopias yields to the largest Tunnies, but if matched against them it would take the prize for strength and courage.

True, the Tunny also is a powerful species of fish, but after its first onset against its adversary and vigorous opponent it forgoes its strength, and as its blood congeals, it very soon surrenders and is then caught.

The Aulopias on the contrary carries on the struggle for a long time when it is attacked with vigour, and withstands the fisherman as it would an adversary, and on most occasions gets the better of him by gathering itself together, bowing its head, and Thrusting down, into the depths ; it has a forceful jaw and a powerful neck and is exceedingly strong.

But when it is captured it is a most beautiful sight: it has wide open eyes, round and large, Such eyes as Homer sings of in oxen. And the jaw, though powerful, as I remarked, contributes to its beauty.

Its back is like the colour of the deepest lapis lazuli, its belly underneath is white. A stripe of a golden hue starts at the head and descending to the region of the tail ends in a circle.

How caught

I wish to speak also of the artifices employed in hunting it which I remember to have heard. The fishermen previously select spots from ,a large area where they suppose the Aulopiae to be congregating and after catching a number of Crow-fish in their bag nets they anchor their boat and maintain a continuous din; the Crow-fish they make fast in a noose and let Out on a line.

Meanwhile the Aulopiae hearing the din and observing the bait, come swimming up from all sides and congregate and circle about the boat. And the din and the quantity of food have such a soothing effect upon them that, even though men reach out their hands, they remain and submit to the human touch because, as I judge, they are slaves to food, and in fact, as their pursuers maintain, because their strength gives them confidence.

There are also tame ones among them which the fishermen recognize as their benefactors and comrades, so with them they maintain a truce.

And another strange fishes follow them like leaders, and these aliens, as one might call them, the men hunt and kill, but the tame fish, which may be likened to decoy-doves, they do not hunt but spare, nor would any prudent fisherman ever be reduced to such straits as to catch a fame Aulopias deliberately, for if by some mischance one happens to be caught it brings trouble.

The fish is captured either by being pierced with a hook or by being mortally wounded.

We see bird-catchers also abstaining from killing birds that decoy others, whether for sale or for the table. There are other methods besides of catching these fish.

19. The royal parks of India and their birds

In the royal residences in India where the greatest of the kings of that country lives, there are so many objects for admiration that neither their birds Memnon's city of Susa with all its extravagance, nor the magnificence of Ecbatana is to be compared with them.

(These places appear to be the pride of Persia, if there is to be any comparison between the two countries.) The remaining splendours it is not the purpose of this narrative to detail ; but in the parks tame peacocks and pheasants are kept, and they live in the cultivated shrubs to which the royal gardeners pay due attention.

Moreover there are shady groves and herbage growing among them, and the boughs are interwoven by the woodman's art. And what is more remarkable about the climate of the country, the actual trees are of the evergreen type, and their leaves never grow old and fall: some of them are indigenous, others have been imported from abroad after careful consideration.

And these, the olive alone excepted, are, an ornament to the place and, enhance its beauty. India does not bear the olive of its own accord, nor if it comes from elsewhere, does it foster its growth.

20. The Parrot

Well, there are other birds besides, free and unenslaved, which come of their own accord and make their beds and resting-places in these trees. There too Parrots are kept and crowd around the king.

But no Indian eats a Parrot in spite of their great numbers, the reason being that the Brahmins regard them as sacred and even place them above all other birds. And they add that they are justified in so doing, for the Parrot is the only bird that gives the most convincing imitation of human speech.

There are also in these royal domains beautiful lakes, the work of man's hands, which contain fish of immense size and tame. And nobody hunts them, only the king's sons during their childhood; and in calm waters, quite free from danger, they fish and sport and even learn the art of sailing as well.

21. Fishing for Mullet

In the Ionian sea off Leucatas and in the waters round Actium (the country there they call Epirus) abound, swimming, so to say, in companies and vast multitudes. These fish are hunted, and in a most astounding manner.

The method is as follows. The local fishermen watch for a moonless night and after supper pair off and launch a skiff while there is neither wave nor swell but the sea is calm, and then row forward quietly by slow degrees.

One of the men gently agitates the water with his oar, propelling the boat step by step, so to speak, while the other propped on his elbow weighs down his end of the boat, depressing it until the gunwale is nearly at the water-level. And the Mullet and others of their kind, either because they enjoy the night or because they delight in the calm, quit their holes and lairs, swim up, and show the tip of their head above the water and are so occupied in swimming to the surface that they draw near to the shore.

So the fishermen observing this begin to sail, and the rush of the boat starts a gentle ripple. Therefore the fish in fleeing from the shore turn and owing to their numbers jostle one another into the portion of the boat sloping toward them, and once inside are caught.

22. The Trochus

Sea-monsters of excessive bulk and of prodigious size swim in mid-ocean, and are at times struck by lightning. Besides these there are others of the same kind that come close to the shore and their name is Trochus (wheel).

These swim in droves, especially on the right side of Thracian Athos and in the bays as one sails from Sigeum, and one may encounter them along the mainland opposite, close to what is called the Tomb of Artachaees and the isthmus of Acanthus where the canal which the Persian King cut through Athos is to be seen.

And they say that these monsters which they call Trochus are timid, though they expose their crest and spines of enormous length so that they are often seen above the water. But at the sound of oars they revolve and contract and plunge as deep as they can go.

It is from this, you see, that they derive their name. And again they uncoil and with a rolling motion swim up to the surface.

23. The Triton

Concerning Tritons, while fishermen assert that they have no clear account or positive proof of their existence, yet there is a report very widely circulated of certain monsters in the sea, of human shape from the head down to the waist.

And Demostratus in his treatise on fishing says that at Tanagra he has seen a Triton in pickle. It was, he says, in most respects as portrayed in statues and pictures, but its head had been so marred by time and was so far from distinct that it was not easy to make it out or recognize it.' And when I touched it there fell from it rough scales, quite hard and resistant.

And a member of the Council, one of those chosen by lot to regulate the affairs of Greece and entrusted with the government for a single year, intending to test and prove the nature of what he saw, removed a small piece of the skin and burnt it in the fire; whereupon a noisome smell from the burning object thrown into the flames assailed the nostrils of the bystanders.

But' he says,' we were unable to guess whether the creature was born on land or in the sea. The experiment however cost him dear, for shortly afterwards he lost his life while crossing a small, narrow strait in a short, six-oared ferry-boat.

And the inhabitants of Tanagra maintained,' so he says, 'that this befell ,him because he profaned the Triton, and they declared that when he was, taken lifeless from the sea he disgorged a fluid which smelt like the hide of the Triton at the time when the man cast it into the fire and burnt it.

As to the quarter from which the Triton strayed and how he came to be cast ashore here, the inhabitants of Tanagra and Demostratus must explain. In view of these facts I bow to the god, and a witness of such authority claims our belief; and Apollo of Didyma must be a sufficient guarantee to every man of sound mind and strong intelligence. At any rate he says that the Triton is a creature of the sea, and his words are: A child of Poseidon, portent of the waters, a clear-voiced Triton, encountered as he swam the rush of a hollow vessel. If then the omniscient god says that Tritons do exist, we should entertain no doubts on the subject.

Get All The Books In The Series:

Animal Peculiarity Volume 1 Part [1-8]
Animal Peculiarity Volume 2 Part [1-8]
Animal Peculiarity Volume 3 Part [1-8]